RICHARD SCHOOL

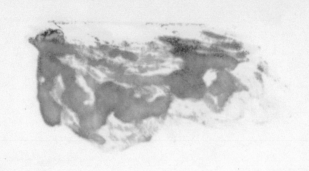

LEE

THE GALLANT GENERAL

By JEANETTE EATON
Illustrated by Harry Daugherty

WILLIAM MORROW AND COMPANY
New York · 1953

. .

THE BIG CLOCK in the church tower of Alexandria struck three. The slow strokes could be heard from one end of the little Virginia town to the other as it dreamed peacefully on the Potomac River. Suddenly the quiet of dusty streets was split by the shouts and laughter of boys who came rushing out of school.

"Robert!" one of them shouted to a tall lad who was walking rapidly away. "Robert Lee! Come swimming with us."

3

Robert turned toward them. "I'm off to market," he said. "Then I have to see to the stables."

His schoolmates stared. "Well," cried another, "you act like the head of the house."

Robert grinned. "So I am," he said. "But every day isn't as busy as this one. I'll meet you at the river tomorrow."

In that year of 1819, Robert Edward Lee was twelve years old. His father, once an officer on General Washington's staff during the Revolution, had died the year before. His mother was not well and could do no more than look after her two little girls, so she depended on Robert to manage the household. This he did with a quiet skill that won admiration from all her friends.

From childhood until his late teens Robert never went outside the boundaries of Virginia. Nor did he wish to. He enjoyed hunting, swimming, sailing, and riding. He thought Virginia, with its blue hills, pine woods, and wide rivers, must be the most beautiful land in the world.

At nineteen, Robert E. Lee entered the United States Military Academy at West Point, New York. He chose to be an engineer. That meant map drawing, special work in mathematics, and learning how to build bridges and forts. Although he stood at the head of his class and never had one black mark for misbehavior, he was not conceited. The other cadets liked him for his lively sense of fun.

June 30, 1831, was a glorious day for the young lieutenant. He had graduated from West Point two

years before and was serving his country as an army engineer. The pay was small. But on that day he felt very rich, for he was marrying a lovely bride— Mary Custis. The Custis home, Arlington, stood on a high bluff above the Potomac, across the river from Washington.

For several years Lieutenant Lee was sent here and there to work on forts along the Atlantic coast or on flood control of rivers. His wife often went with him. Even after they had a family of three boys and four girls, they managed to be together much of the time.

In the summer of 1846, however, a letter came to Lee from Washington that ended his peaceful family life. "I'm ordered to Mexico!" Lee told his wife. "It's war. I'm leaving tomorrow."

Custis, the oldest boy, cried, "But why is the United States going to fight Mexico?"

Lee tried to explain. Ten years before, American settlers had taken Texas from Mexico by force. Now a quarrel had started over boundaries. A force of 4000 United States soldiers, sent down to protect the border, was attacked by Mexicans. At once the United States declared war. Our government had long wanted an excuse to acquire by conquest some of the land owned by Mexico in the West and Southwest.

Captain Lee joined the large forces of General Winfield Scott, commander of the American army, and they landed near Vera Cruz in March, 1847.

Fighting began at once, and in the very first

7

battles Lee made his mark by his skillful placing of the batteries and guns and his successful direction of the firing. General Scott put him on his staff and made him a major.

Five months later, the American army had fought its way to within a few miles of Mexico City. Then the General gave Lee a special mission. "Major," said Scott, "I want you to find a route to the city that will bypass the enemy positions."

Lee believed such a pass could be found through a strange waste land called the Pedrigal. Thousands of years before, volcanoes had flung down enormous blocks of lava over three square miles of the valley north of the capital. Between giant stones gaped deep ravines filled with cactus, prickly pear, and thorn trees. Lee rode into this wild place with a small body of soldiers and then went galloping back to headquarters.

"General," he reported, "there's a good mule track through the Pedrigal. If we widen it, we can take artillery and troops across and come out on a smooth road to Mexico City."

The portly General puffed with satisfaction. "We'll surprise the enemy. Take five hundred men tomorrow at dawn and make us a road."

By afternoon of the next day, three miles of rough road were ready, and an advance body of soldiers came marching along. Lee guided the officer in command. At sunset they were attacked from two directions by Mexican forces. Only night and a fierce storm saved them.

"I must have more troops at once," said the officer. "But how can I send word to General Scott? No one could get through the Pedrigal at night in this storm."

"I think I can, sir," said Lee quietly.

With four soldiers, he started back across the lava field. It would have been a difficult march even by daylight. In the black darkness, through torrents of rain, it was almost impossible. Some-how, Lee kept his men together, and at last they reached the outpost camp, exhausted. Lee had to tramp three more miles to the General's head-quarters.

He spent the whole night leading troops with cannon and supplies back through the Pedrigal. At dawn the guns were roaring. Now it was the Mexicans who were between two fires, and by nightfall the Americans had a clear road to Mexico City.

"Splendid work, Major Lee!" boomed the General that evening. "You have shown great courage! I shall ask that you be made a colonel, sir."

It took twenty-five days to prepare for the battle against Mexico City. Enemy troops were massed at the east gates. To the west, the city was defended by a mighty fortress with walls so steep they could be scaled only by the use of ladders.

On September 13, 1847, the attack began at dawn, and Lee was in the thick of it. Every shift of guns was made by his orders, and before night the fortress was captured.

Next day, bands played triumphantly while General Scott rode into the Grand Plaza. American soldiers cheered wildly when the conquest of Mexico was solemnly proclaimed.

In the midst of the hubbub a young lieutenant spoke to Lee. "Major, who is that man over there at the head of his company? Yesterday he fought like a wildcat."

Glancing toward the fountain, Lee saw a black-browed young officer who had an air of scorning this scene of victory. "I met him a few days ago," said Lee. "His name is Ulysses S. Grant."

After Mexico signed the treaty of peace, Lee could return to his family, and in 1852 he was appointed commander of the United States Military Academy. For three years the family lived happily together at West Point on the Hudson River.

Mary's father died in 1857. Then Lee was given leave from duties in the South to settle the Custis

estate at Arlington. He read one item in his father-in-law's will with excitement and deep satisfaction. All his life Lee had hated slavery. That any man could own another human being seemed to him a denial of Christ's teaching. Mr. Custis had willed that all his slaves be set free.

Like most Americans in those years, Lee was unhappy about his country. No longer was there peace or brotherhood in the land. A gulf was growing wider month by month between the people in the South and those in the North.

This split came partly from different ways of life. Northerners were building big cities, factories, ships. Southerners lived in small towns or on plantations where they raised cotton, tobacco, and rice. In the South, men were loyal first of all to their own states rather than to the nation as a whole. Northerners, on the other hand, fiercely believed that only a firm union could keep the country great and prosperous.

Beneath all these differences lay one mighty

quarrel—the question of slavery. Planters declared that Negro slaves were necessary to work their big cotton and rice fields. Some Southern leaders dreamed of a cotton empire, founded on slavery, that would stretch from the Atlantic Ocean to the Pacific. These men had begun to say they wished to separate from the Northern states.

About these great questions Robert E. Lee made his own feeling clear. He had always served his country and loved the Union with devotion. "It would be a terrible disaster," he said, "if this nation were divided. Slavery must go as soon as possible. But the rich North does not understand that millions have been spent on slaves and such a change will take time."

Many Southerners boiled with anger when they read what some Northern writers were saying—that slavery ought to be abolished by law right away. People who believed this were called abolitionists.

There came a day in October, 1859, when it seemed as if one of these abolitionists would involve the whole country in war. His name was John Brown. With a small party, he seized the government arsenal at Harpers Ferry, a little town in West Virginia. Brown held the townsfolk at bay and sent out a call to Negro slaves to come, seize arms from the arsenal, and set up their own republic.

It was late at night when Lee heard of this astonishing affair. General Scott sent for him to come to Washington and told him the story. "Colonel Lee," said Scott, "take a regiment of marines and start tonight for Harpers Ferry. This rebellion must be put down at once."

Next morning Lee and his marines reached Harpers Ferry. He learned that Brown had captured six citizens and was holding them as hostages in a building he was using as a fortress. Lee ordered a few men to break down the doors with rams, but to use no guns. In fifteen minutes the invaders were captured and the hostages set free.

When Lee saw the old leader, with his burning eyes and wild gray hair, stride proudly forth, he felt a sudden throb of sympathy for him. John Brown was hanged as a rebel, but because he risked everything to rid the nation of slavery, he became a kind of mad hero to many people in the North.

After that, abolitionists were feared and detested in the South more than ever. But Colonel Lee, who was sent down to Texas to check Indian raids, thought many settlers there were as dangerous to the nation as John Brown. Texans often told him that the South should form a separate nation. "That

RICHARD SCHOOL

would mean civil war!" Lee protested in horror. "We could lick the Yankees in a few weeks," they replied.

Stormy feeling spread over the country in 1860. A new party calling itself Republican nominated an Illinois lawyer, Abraham Lincoln, for President. His speeches made him friends in the North, enemies in the South. He declared that slavery must not spread westward and that the Union must not, could not, be broken. Southern politicians swore that if Lincoln was elected, the Southern states would leave the Union.

Lee read the news with despair. "Secession from the Union is rebellion," he wrote his family. "True, the North has been violent and unfair. But our ancestors who framed the Constitution never dreamed it could be broken at will." Lee's own ancestors had helped found the nation, and his soul cried out against the destruction that seemed to be coming upon it.

Lincoln was elected President in November,

1860. At once Southern politicians began to carry out their threats. Before Christmas, South Carolina left the Union. By the time Lincoln took his oath of office in March, 1861, six more states had seceded — Mississippi, Florida, Alabama, Georgia, Louisiana, and Texas. They formed the Confederate States of America and elected Senator Jefferson Davis as their president. Lee soon learned that Texans were seizing government forts and arsenals, and he guessed that was happening in each Confederate state. Then came orders from General Scott, calling him to Washington.

During the journey north, he spent hours in tormented question. Would Virginia secede? His beloved Virginia! Could he ever desert his own state? To all the excited questions that were hurled at him on his arrival at home, Lee answered simply, "I am waiting to see what Virginia decides."

Suddenly, in April, every American was forced to take sides. Violence exploded in South Carolina. State troops had fired on Fort Sumter, a United States fort near Charleston. Six days later the fort had to surrender. The next day President Lincoln called for 75,000 volunteers to defend the Union and all its properties. War had begun.

Mary Lee watched her husband anxiously. His face looked pale and drawn. "The Virginia convention has been meeting a long time," he said. "I can think of nothing but the final vote. Will our state secede?"

Then came the news of the vote—Virginia had left the Union. After supper that evening Lee shut himself in his study. Here it was, he thought—the moment he had dreaded for months. Head in hands, he reviewed all that he had felt. He loved the Union and hated slavery. How could he hesitate? From his lips came a groan of anguish. Then in a flash, the decision was made. He found that one supreme loyalty had always held his heart.

23

At midnight he went to join his wife. The tired eyes in his haggard face met hers calmly. In his hand were two letters. "I've written my resignation to the War Department, Mary," he said quietly, "and my regrets to General Scott." As she flung her arms about him, he added, "Virginia will be invaded and I could never be her foe."

Two days later, Robert E. Lee bade his wife and daughters good-by. A telegram from the Governor of Virginia had called him to Richmond. Lee was calm and cheerful, for his duty was clear to him. Before midnight of that same day he had put on the gray Confederate uniform. The Governor had made him a brigadier general in charge of Virginia's defense.

Richmond was in a frenzy. President Lincoln had ordered the state troops of the South to return peacefully to their homes within twenty days, so people believed that invasion would start in three weeks. Lee sent militia to guard railroad centers and to strengthen forts along the big rivers and

the sea coast. Volunteers were pouring into the city, and officers began drilling them.

"What an odd lot they are!" laughed Lee. But his eyes shone with pride. Youths in new gray uniforms were mounted on high-bred horses. Behind them came uneven lines of bearded farmers in blue jeans, carrying squirrel guns. The General's two older sons, Custis and Rooney, had already enlisted in the Confederate army.

Soon Virginia joined the Confederacy. Rich-

mond was made the capital and, late in June, President Jefferson Davis arrived with the entire government. Davis made Lee his military adviser, and together they faced their terrible problems. The South had almost no factories. Where were cannon, muskets, shoes, uniforms, and ammunition to come from? "European nations will send us these supplies," said Davis. "They need our cotton. But Federal ships will try to blockade our ports."

For two months Virginians learned about the

war only from newspapers. Most of the fighting was far off in Missouri. Three more states had joined the Confederacy—Arkansas, North Carolina, and Tennessee—and now eleven opposed the twenty-three Northern states. Members of the Confederate congress were sure the North would promptly sue for peace. Almost gleefully they learned in July that a Federal army was about to move south from Washington to invade Virginia.

Lee advised President Davis to mass his troops at a railroad junction in northern Virginia. "That will be the goal of the invaders," he said.

Near the junction flowed a creek called Bull Run, and the first important battle of the war was named for it. Lee longed to have a part in the fight, but duties kept him in Richmond. The first reports telegraphed from the front made him heartsick. Southern troops were losing. But suddenly crowds near the telegraph office were cheering wildly. "We've licked 'em!" they shouted. "The Yankees are on the run!"

So they were. Frightened, defeated, the Federal army fled in panic. Guns, blankets, and knapsacks were strewn for miles in its wake. Lee shared the rejoicing. But that evening at the railroad station he watched trainloads of dead and wounded come in and saw the weeping women on the platform. The sight smote his heart. This was no foreign war. It was here in the midst of America. Brothers were fighting one another. Many of the young men carried past him on stretchers were sons of his own dear friends.

In spite of this first victory, Lee was well aware of the odds against the Confederacy. The South had no navy and the Southern sea coast would be controlled by Federal warships. The Union, with four times the white population of the South, could raise mighty armies to attack forts along the western rivers and to invade Virginia. Southern factories were just starting to make the things needed in war.

President Davis talked over these facts with Lee early in March, 1862. "We can still get food from

the West," said Davis, "if we control the rivers. But two of our forts have been taken on the Cumberland and Tennessee Rivers and that fighting devil, General Grant, is moving on Fort Shiloh."

Always at the sound of that name there flashed before Lee's eyes the square in Mexico City and the frowning young officer. Now the lieutenant was a powerful general.

A body of Confederate troops was now ordered to chase the Union forces out of the Shenandoah Valley west of Richmond. The commander was Thomas J. Jackson, a general who had won fame at the battle of Bull Run and a nickname loved by his men. To rally a frightened brigade, an officer had shouted, "Look at General Jackson, standing like a stone wall!" Now Jackson set off confidently on his mission.

In May, the huge Federal army in southern Virginia moved up to a position near Richmond. It was reported that more reinforcements were coming from Washington. There was even worse

news for the confederacy. General Grant had captured Fort Shiloh, a key point on the Tennessee
River, and Admiral Farragut had taken the great
port of New Orleans.

When Stonewall Jackson's reports came in, he
became the hero of the day. In one month's time,
by fast marches, surprise attacks, and swift retreats,
he had won five battles and captured hundreds of
guns and prisoners. He whirled so near Washington
as to throw panic into the government. The 40,000
soldiers ready to join the attack on Richmond were
held back to defend the national capital. Jackson
then rushed to join the defense of Richmond.

On May 31, Union and Confederate forces met
at the Chickahominy River, a few miles east of the
city. President Davis and General Lee rode out
from the capital to watch the battle. The action
was badly planned and it ended in confusion for the
Southern troops. On the ride back to Richmond,
Davis said suddenly, "General Lee, I shall assign
you to the command of this army."

Glad to be at last in the thick of action, Lee gave out his orders of the day to the "Army of Northern Virginia," his new name for the troops. They liked it and cheered their commander.

Lee selected General J. E. B. Stuart, commander of Confederate cavalry, for a scouting expedition. Ordered by Lee to get all possible information about the Union army, the handsome young officer chose 1200 men for the task. Among them was Rooney Lee.

That expedition made history. Stuart's horsemen rode clear around the Union army, captured many horses, and brought back complete information about the size of the army and its probable line of march. Thus aided, Lee was ready by June 25 to meet the Union forces at the Chickahominy River, north of Richmond.

On the eve of his first great battle, Lee rode around camp for a close look at his soldiers. Most of them had gathered around small fires to cook rations for a three-day campaign. Lee's heart was

torn to hear them singing and laughing, as if no threat of pain and death hung over them.

Hundreds of those boys lost their lives in the fighting that went on for seven days. The battle shifted through swamps and thorny scrub, across shot-torn hollows, and up hillsides manned by murderous guns. When at last it was over, Lee was silent and sad. He had won no victory and his losses were heavy. But the Federal army had suffered heavy losses too, and had been pushed eighteen miles away from Richmond. It was continuing to retreat.

A six weeks' lull allowed troops to rest and officers to gather supplies. Lee joined his wife, who was now in Richmond. Custis also was there, as aide to President Davis. Robert, Lee's youngest son, was training for a gunners' brigade.

Soon reports poured in that another attack was to be made on Richmond that summer, and early in August the fierce struggle began again. Lee brought his army up to the railroad junction near Bull Run, and there, for the second time, was able to inflict a severe defeat on the invaders.

At twilight Lee rode alone over the battlefield to study the day's action. An officer rode up to him. "General," he said, "here is someone who wants to speak to you."

Before Lee could nod assent, a figure in smoke-blackened uniform appeared, and a grimy face looked up at him from the shadows. "What can I do for you, my man?" asked Lee politely.

"Why, General, don't you know me?" the young gunner answered, laughing.

Lee, bending low, exclaimed, "Robert! Bless you, my son! Are you all right?"

"Yes, sir!" answered the young man. "This has been a great day!"

Yes, thought the General as he rode on, but what next? His men were almost starved. The roads were so muddy that it was impossible to drag big guns and wagons in pursuit of the enemy. Yet Lee knew that now he had won the trust of President Davis, of the whole South, and—best of all—of his soldiers. Cheers from the ranks told him what every commander needs to know—that the men were eager to follow his lead.

Before he slept that night, Lee decided to march into Maryland, where many people wanted the South to win and would, he thought, sell him the food he needed. Then he hoped to swing west into Pennsylvania, destroy railroad bridges, and frighten the Federal government into offering peace terms.

That move proved a huge disappointment. People in Maryland were afraid to be friendly to the Confederates. Supplies were hard to get. So the General changed his plan. He sent Jackson and Jeb Stuart with large forces to capture Harpers Ferry and its stores of food and ammunition. Before news came back from them, Lee heard from his scouts that the big Union army was on his trail. So, hastily turning his forces westward in Maryland, he placed them at Antietam Creek, near Sharpsburg, to await the attack.

Then came a messenger from Jackson. "General," he cried, "Harpers Ferry is ours!" Jackson himself joined his chief shortly with troops. But there was no sign of the remaining divisions.

Never had Lee imagined such a struggle as the last day of fighting at Antietam Creek. His troops were outnumbered two to one. Early in the day, one whole Confederate brigade was wrecked by a fierce attack.

From the hill where he was directing action, Lee

sped messengers to his generals. All reserves were to march forward and hold the lines. In a roar of guns and a fog of smoke the Confederates struggled manfully. In wild anxiety Lee watched through field glasses for a sight of the reinforcements. All he saw was a file of ambulances rushing the wounded into Sharpsburg. In the valley the dead were piled in heaps. On the hills were wavering lines of weary men in gray. Must he retreat? Should he surrender?

The sudden sound of bugles drew his tired eyes to a critical spot. A mass of gray uniforms was pushing up the hillside! The troops from Harpers Ferry had come at last. Like demons, they flung themselves upon the enemy. The Union lines broke and drew back. Swiftly, then, the September dusk ended the firing. The battle was over.

By the next afternoon the Army of Northern Virginia had safely crossed the Potomac River into its own country. The soldiers made camp in a high-hearted mood. Their leader had praised them. Courage under deadly fire and stubborn fighting

against heavy odds had proved this army great.

Before the end of 1862, these gallant men won their second smashing victory. A battle at Fredericksburg cost the Union forces the loss of 11,000 soldiers and an equal number of guns. The disabled Union army retreated far from Richmond. With affection and pride the soldiers cheered wildly for "Marse Robert," the name his old Negro servant called General Lee. They cheered for Traveller, too, the Commander's beautiful gray horse.

On New Year's morning, 1863, Lee looked with brave honesty at the future. Yes, he might win more battles, but he could never defeat the North. If the Union lost soldiers, guns, and horses, it could get more. Not so the South. All the soldiers and most of the citizens were hungry.

Never had the General been sure that Europe would support the Confederacy, although many Southerners and their president counted on such help. But on that New Year's Day, President Lincoln signed the famous Emancipation Proclamation, freeing all slaves. From then on, England and other countries were afraid to befriend enemies of the Union. Most European governments had declared themselves against slavery. Now people in other lands linked the North with a fight for human freedom. It was a deadly blow to the South.

January of 1863 was cold in Virginia. Lee returned one day from a ride around camp with tears in his eyes. In a choking voice he said to one of his generals, "Our poor men are almost barefoot and few of them have blankets. It's like the winter at Valley Forge that my father lived through. Yet no one complains. This army has a magnificent spirit."

The soldiers proved that spirit during the first big battle of the year. It took place in May at Chancellorsville, near Fredericksburg. Once more a Union army was marching down toward Richmond, 132,000 strong. Lee had only 60,000 men. Yet he had the courage to divide his forces. Stonewall Jackson marched off with nearly half the army to attack the enemy's right flank.

Never had Lee's men fought more mightily. Never was the rebel yell more terrifying. Before dusk fell, Lee knew he had checked the Federal attack. About midnight he stretched out on a blanket for a bit of rest. After the fearful din of battle the quiet of the sweet May night seemed magical.

"Report from General Jackson, sir!"

Starting awake, Lee blinked at the officer beside him. It was good news. Jackson had half circled the Union right wing and at sunset had made a swift attack. Surprised while they were cooking supper, hundreds of Northern men were captured. With guns blazing, Jackson's troops broke up and scattered the whole division. Long after dark the fight went on through the woods.

"But, sir," stammered the messenger," General Jackson was shot. He is in great danger."

When the officer had gone, Lee groaned to himself in anguish. What would I do without him? he thought. Jackson is my good right arm.

At dawn the Confederates charged the Union positions and by ten o'clock had captured Chancellorsville. Fierce struggles went on all day. But toward evening the Union forces drew off. Lee had defeated an army more than twice the size of his own. Telegrams from every corner of the South congratulated the master of strategy.

The price of that victory, however, put the whole South into mourning. For on May 7, Stonewall Jackson died of his wounds. Lee prayed for strength

45

to meet this tragic loss, but no one could take General Jackson's place.

Urged on by President Davis, Lee now decided to invade the North, hoping to lure the Union army out of Virginia. By the middle of June, the long lines of Confederate troops, supply wagons, and batteries were filing by several routes toward southern Pennsylvania. The soldiers felt like conquerors.

Trudging along the dusty roads, they sang "Dixie" and "Oh! Susanna." They cheered for Marse Robert and shouted boasts that the Yankees were no match for them.

Lee was proud of such spirit. Never had the Army of Northern Virginia been defeated. But in his own heart was a turmoil of questions. Invading unknown country was a fearful risk. He sent two forces northward by different directions to test Union resistance. General Stuart's cavalry remained in the southeast to watch the moves of the Federal army. Day by day Lee expected word from him, but none came. Therefore he had no idea that the Union forces were coming north to head him off.

Toward the end of June the main corps of the Army of Northern Virginia reached Chambersburg, in Pennsylvania. There the Commander learned from spies that the enemy was approaching. At once he sped messengers to recall the two forces he had sent toward the north. He himself, with part of the army, camped on the eastern slope of the Blue Ridge, while one division moved forward.

Early on July 1, Lee rode out to study the lay of the land. All at once he heard the distant sound of cannon. Had a serious battle begun? Surely fighting could be avoided until the whole Confederate army was rounded up! Lee spurred Traveller forward. A few miles farther on he learned the truth. A desperate fight was going on in and around a

small town cradled in the hills. The great and terrible battle of Gettysburg had begun.

That day the Confederates had the advantage. Union troops were driven both from the north of Gettysburg and from a long ridge northwest of it. But at the end of the day and during the night, Union brigades were stationed on Cemetery Ridge and Culps Hill, positions commanding both the town and the countryside around. Lee took his position along Seminary Ridge, facing the fields which rolled gently up to the Federal posts.

This unexpected battle forced Lee to take the offensive, for he could not afford to be pushed back into the mountain passes. On July 2, he ordered action to begin at dawn. But orders were confused, and it was four o'clock in the afternoon before the guns began to blaze. Then the summer day grew dark with smoke. Brave Texans made charge after charge against a high mound called Little Round Top, but they were mowed down each time. Amid the rocks below, soldiers fought a hand-to-hand battle. A Confederate attack on Cemetery Ridge was pushed back with fearful losses on both sides. Not until the moon was up did fighting stop and the work of rescuing the wounded begin. Lee rode from division to division to encourage men and officers. His desperate anxiety lifted when Stuart and his cavalry arrived.

Dawn of July 3 was greeted by a tremendous fire from Federal guns upon the Confederate posts. The Southerners then tried to charge their enemies, but whole brigades were wiped out. For six hours fight-

ing continued on the northern section of the lines. When there came a lull, Lee called his generals together for a council of war among the trees on Seminary Ridge. He told them that the only remaining hope was to strike the Union forces at the center. Attacks both on the right and the left had failed. Ammunition was getting low. It was a choice between this last effort or retreat.

"We must take Cemetery Ridge by storm," said Lee.

General Pickett's five thousand men, who were fresh and rested, were chosen to be the spearhead of the drive. Ten thousand other troops were to advance on either side. All had to cross an open meadow three quarters of a mile wide, then rush the ridge. At a signal, more than one hundred Confederate cannon blazed forth. For a long time Federal cannon returned the fire. At last came dead silence, then a shouted command to the Confederate troops. "Forward!"

With flags flying, the columns started. The soldiers marched in perfect order. Stern and breathless, Lee, seated on Traveller, watched from Seminary Ridge. Now the first lines were halfway across the field. Not a shot opposed them. Then all at once from the ridge ahead came shot and shell upon the ranks. They did not waver. Lines of men were mowed down like wheat. Wounded horses, screaming with pain, flung officers to the ground. Still the brigades marched on. Each moment the ranks grew thinner. But at last Confederate soldiers were charging up the slope and over the stone wall on top.

Pistol shots, bayonets, and musket butts met them there. For an instant the Union men were driven back. But half the Southern troops lay dead or dying in the meadow.

Lee watched the action in despair. Deep in his heart he knew this was the turning point of the war. For he had lost the battle of Gettysburg.

A few last clashes took place that day. In the night Lee marshaled all his troops along Seminary Ridge. But behind the front lines the retreat was preparing. Rain began to fall, and under its veil the Army of Northern Virginia started its homeward march.

On that same day another Union victory was won in the West. Ulysses S. Grant captured Vicksburg, and the great Mississippi River was in Northern hands. The Confederacy was shrinking.

"We'll hold Virginia!" Lee told his generals.

His brave words lightened the darkness of that agonizing retreat. Rain, weariness, hunger—these were nothing compared to the horrible shadow of Federal pursuit. Whenever Lee cantered to a hilltop and looked down on his army, he could see mile after mile of slowly moving supply wagons and carts with wounded, of batteries and troops. How helpless that army looked! The crawling caravan would need ten days to reach the Potomac River and cross into Virginia.

At last, all that was left of the Confederate army reached the Potomac—only to find the river so swollen with rain that crossing was impossible. There was nothing to do but camp and wait. Lee knew that if the Union army fell upon them there, it might be the end.

Meanwhile, with frenzied energy scouts brought boats and built a shaky bridge. On the 13th of July the slow crossing began. Supply wagons and the wounded went first. After dusk the infantry took up the march. All night, by the light of torches, the crossing went on.

Even after daylight on the 14th, the enemy was not in sight. The last brigades marched over the bridge. The boats were removed. Then and only then did the powerful Union divisions come marching to the river. Too late! The Army of Northern Virginia was safe in its own land.

No paradise lay before it, however. The countryside was swept bare of food. Farms were ruined and villages empty. Yet all that fall of 1863, the troops struggled successfully against the invaders.

In 1864, Ulysses S. Grant, now chief of all the Federal armies, took the field in Virginia. Mighty guns and massed troops pounded away month by month at the Confederate army. Only Lee's brilliant generalship and the devotion of his men made it possible to withstand the Union assaults. By the beginning of 1865 only one other army of the South was in action—General Johnston's army in North Carolina.

Calmly Lee faced the disaster he could not escape. In early April he warned President Davis that Richmond could be defended no longer. To prevent their capture by the enemy, ammunition factories and stores were set afire. The fire spread through street after street until the city was a smoldering ruin.

Acting on orders from Davis, Lee made heroic efforts to fight his way west to the mountains of Virginia. Every move was blocked. Every skirmish with the enemy ended in the death or capture of thousands of his men.

On Palm Sunday, April 9, 1865, the dawn had not yet come when Lee left his tent. As if ready for parade, the General wore a fine new uniform and polished boots. His shining sword was held by a scarlet sash.

At that moment Confederate guns began to thunder. As Lee stepped forward, two orderlies, galloping up from opposite directions, dismounted before him. They reported that one Confederate

corps was surrounded and that a huge Federal force was ready to attack another.

It was light now, but fog hid the fields. Slowly, as if each word were torn from him, the General said to the officers beside him, "There is nothing left for me to do but go and see General Grant. I would rather die a thousand deaths." His voice shook as he spoke. His face showed the torture he had suffered all night long. He alone was responsible for the fate of his loyal troops, and now the time had come when the dreadful decision could no longer be avoided.

Through shocked silence came the voice of his artillery chief. "General, we can fight on as guerillas in the woods. Surrender the Army of Northern Virginia? Never, sir!"

Lee's eyes blazed. Sternly he said, "Would you have brave men steal food, live like animals, forget their families? No!" He broke off with a start. "Look there, gentlemen!"

The sun was up. The fog had lifted. From the

slope where they stood, they saw beyond the thin Confederate lines a mass of blue uniforms stretching in the distance like the waves of a sea. Lee nodded curtly. He had made his fateful decision. To a young officer he said, "Would you be so good as to accompany me to General Grant?"

Before an hour had passed, all firing had ceased by consent of the commanders of both armies. Down the quiet roads, touched by fringes of spring green, Lee rode on Traveller. The meeting place was at Appomattox Courthouse.

Presently the two great generals were shaking hands. Robert E. Lee faced the short, stooped commander of the Union armies. Unshaven, in a rumpled uniform, Grant murmured that, having been on the battlefield since dawn, he had had no time to dress. They talked a little about the Mexican War. Then, quietly, Lee asked for the terms of surrender. Grant sat down at a table, wrote with a pencil on a piece of paper, and handed it to the Virginian.

As he read, Lee glanced at his victor with a flash of relief. Generous feeling lay behind these terms. No prisoners were to be taken. Officers and men, on their word of honor to preserve the peace, were to keep their swords and pistols and go straight home. Only one protest did Lee make. It would not be fair for officers only to keep their horses. Many soldiers in cavalry and artillery brigades owned their own horses.

"I suppose," mused Grant, "they will need them on the farms. Well, General, let your officers know that any man who owns a horse or mule may ride it home."

In a warm voice Lee said, "This will have a very happy effect on the men." He was also grateful to his victor for ordering a large supply of food to be sent to the starving Confederate troops.

Signed, sealed, and handed to Grant, was the surrender of the Army of Northern Virginia. Still controlling his bitter grief, Lee shook hands with the Union commander and left the house. As he rode back to his own camp, he gathered up all his strength to meet the waiting thousands—his devoted comrades in battle.

All knew what had happened. They crowded around him. Many were sobbing. Some shouted that the war should go on. Others pressed close, trying to stammer out their farewells. By a mighty effort he thanked everyone quietly. At last he was alone in his tent.

Swiftly he reviewed the past four years—moments of glory, hours of excitement, days of fearful anxiety. Now in his mouth was the acid taste of defeat. With a passionate prayer for strength to accept it, he made himself repeat the lesson all Southerners now had to learn: "The struggle is over. A new life will begin, and the wounds of the South must be healed."

Lee rode back to Richmond the next day, and that very evening he heard the news of President Lincoln's death by the hands of an assassin. Like many Southerners, he failed to share the horror and grief of the North. Other miseries crowded upon him. Almost every day he had visits from sick and penniless Confederate soldiers, from men needing jobs, from young fellows asking in despair, "What am I to do?" To all he gave the same advice: "Go home. Help build up the South again."

It was not long before the General received offers of well-paid business positions, which he refused. But an invitation to become president of a small college in Virginia appealed to him, and this was the offer Lee accepted. With quiet happiness he began his work as president of Washington College at Lexington.

In many ways Lee set an example to the bitter, poor, and heartbroken Southerners. He was among the first to take the oath of allegiance to the Union demanded of all important men in the Confederacy. Then up and down the South, men said, "If General Lee took this Yankee oath, I reckon I'd better take it too."

Lee began, in that first summer of peace, a crusade which ended only with his death. "Be true

Americans. Support the Union. Let bygones be bygones. Work for the good of the whole nation." That was the message he spoke and wrote to hundreds of men and women. No one could be rude to a Northerner in his presence without a gentle reproof.

During the first years of peace a torrent of evils poured over the Southern states. Without Lincoln's strong, patient hands to control it, the Congress of the United States, with a huge majority from the North, passed cruel laws of vengeance against the South. Unscrupulous men hurried down there to cheat and rob the people. They put their own judges in the courts, and Southerners found it hard to get justice. But they still listened to their adored general, who said, "Be patient! Things will right themselves in time."

On the few trips he took about the South, Lee was welcomed like a conquering hero. On his only long journey by train people crowded to stations to wave and cheer. Bowing to them from the train

platform, he snatched this chance to spread the gospel of brotherhood. "We are one nation now, my friends. Let us rebuild our land and think only of bringing peace and plenty to our country."

Because they trusted Lee so deeply, they accepted the truth of his words, which spread to the far cor-

ners of the South. Many people in the North learned of his quiet work of healing. When he died on October 10, 1870, Northerners grieved. Newspapers printed warm praise of this outstanding leader.

Robert Edward Lee has gone down in history

as a master of military campaigns. Far more important was his vast influence after the war. His name
stands for generosity of spirit in both small and
critical moments of life. He was a great-hearted,
gallant, and patriotic American.